BOOK ONE

WORLD'S FAVORITE MASTERWORKS FOR CLARINET
Compiled by JAY ARNOLD

This volume contains some of the finest etudes ever written for the clarinet, combined with the complete 1st Clarinet parts to three outstanding symphonic works for orchestra. These clarinet parts may be used to great advantage for play-along study by working with records of these important compositions. Also included is the clarinet part for a very important solo.

	CONTENTS	Page

TWENTY-SIX EXERCISES

FRITZ KROEPSCH

2

7

8

11

12

13

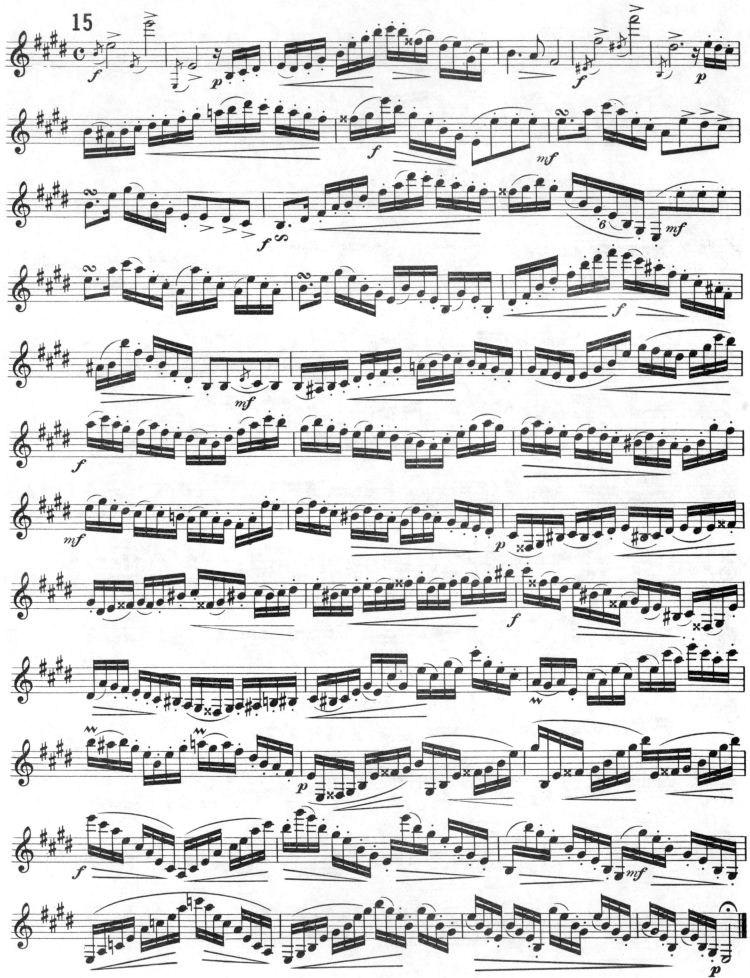

17

18

23

24

26

THIRTY CAPRICES

ERNESTO CAVALLINI

Allegro moderato

34

3 Agitato

Adagio

38

Andante mosso

7

48

e cosí tutto lo studio.

THEME

Moderato

13

Allegro assai

14

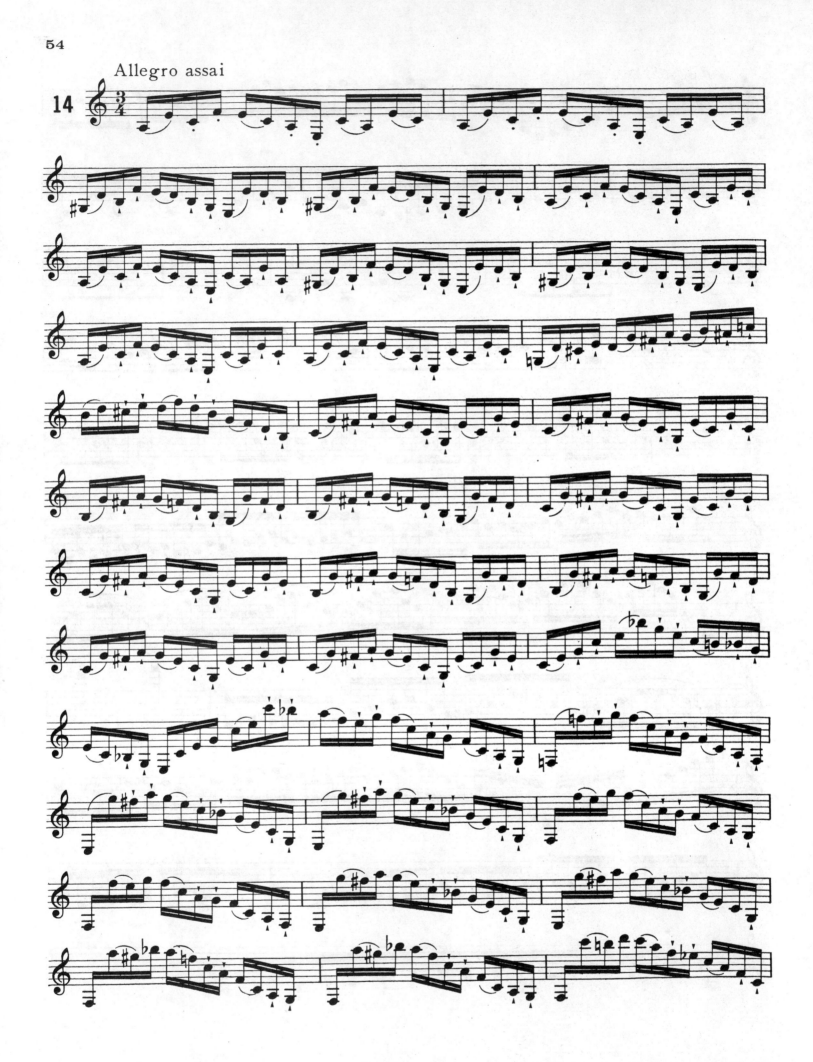

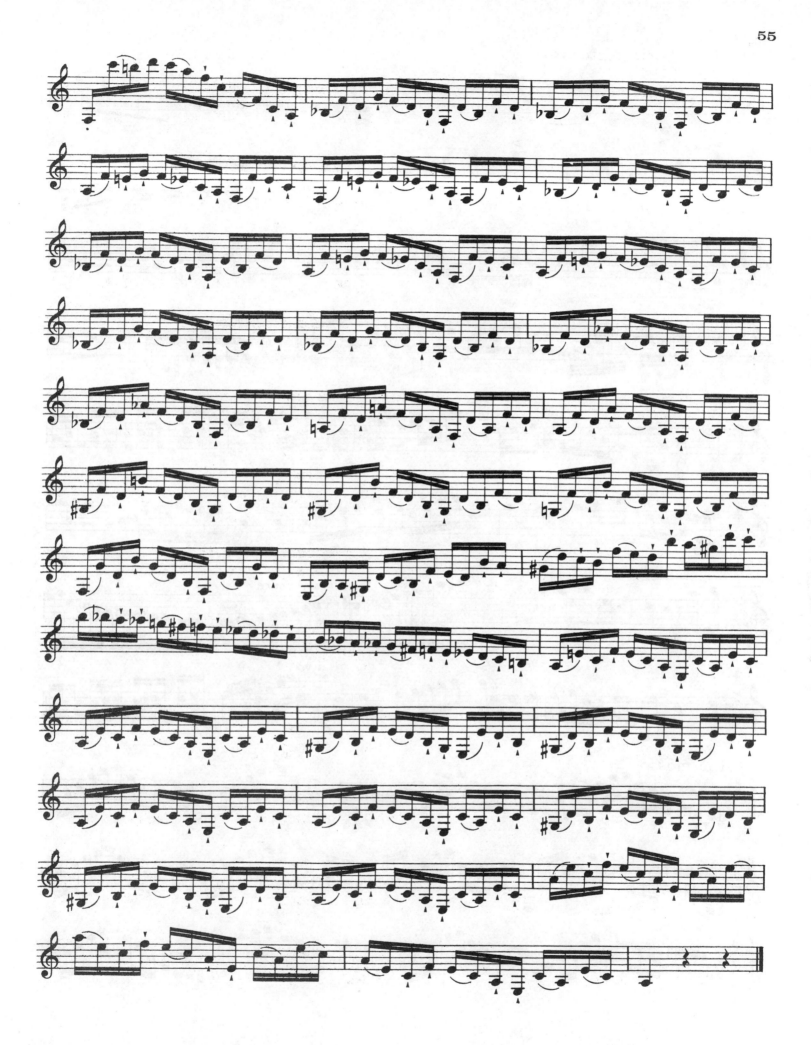

Adagio sostenuto

15

dolce

f

a piacere

f

Più mosso

Maestoso

17

risoluto

a piacere

Allegretto

18

accel.

a piacere

Allegro.

Tempo I

a piacere

Allegro

pp

64

19 Moderato

Più mosso

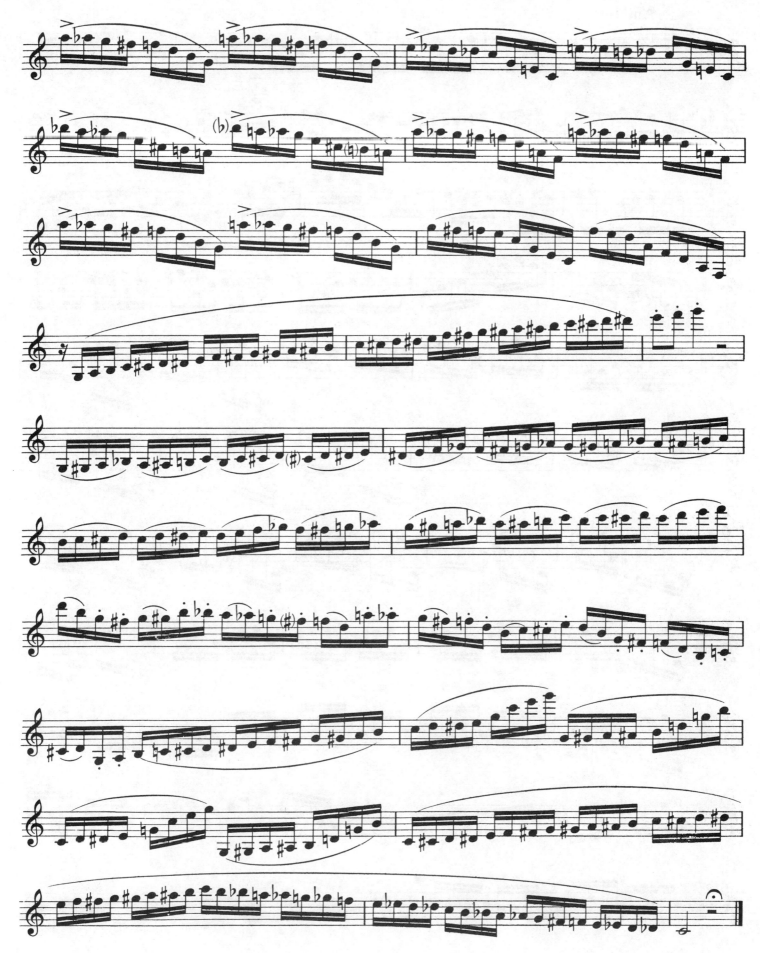

Andante

20

Adagio sostenuto

21

22

Andantino

Allegro mosso

Tempo I

VAR. IV

Allegro risoluto

25

string.

82

Allegro

26

29

dolce

SUITE FROM THE OPERA
LE COQ D'OR
Clarinetto I in B e A

I

NICHOLAS RIMSKY-KORSAKOFF

Clarinetto I in B e A

Clarinetto I in B e A

II

Clarinetto I in B e A

Clarinetto I in B e A

Allegro assai

IV

in A

in B

(muta in B)

Clarinetto I in B e A

Clarinetto I in B e A.

CAPRICCIO ESPAGNOL

Clarinetto I

I ALBORADA

NICHOLAS RIMSKY-KORSAKOFF. Op. 34

in A
Vivo e strepitoso

attacca

Clarinetto I
II VARIAZIONI

III ALBORADA

Clarinetto I

IV SCENA E CANTO GITANO

Clarinetto I

Clarinetto I

V FANDANGO ASTURIANO

Clarinetto I

SYMPHONY NO. 6
(PATHETIQUE)

KLARINETTE I in A

I

PETER I. TSCHAIKOWSKY, Op. 74

II

Allegro con grazia

III

CONCERTINO

SOLO Bb CLARINET

CARL MARIA von WEBER, Op. 26